Awakening The Beauty Of Your Inner Light

How to Find Peace and Joy in Every Moment

Written By
J. M. Thorne

Spiritual wellness is a crucial aspect of overall well-being. It refers to the ability to find meaning and purpose in life, having a clear set of beliefs, and living in accordance with your morals, values, and ethics 1. Essentially, it means understanding and having a clear definition of what's important in life and what's wrong and right and living according to this understanding 1.

There are several practices that can help improve spiritual wellness. Here are some of them:

1. Meditation: Meditation practices refer to a broad collection of activities that seek to focus the mind. For example, we can focus on our breathing, a meaningful word of our choice, the movement of light on the floor as it comes through a window, the sound of a bird, sensations of emotional or physical pain, a text that holds spiritual significance, the kindness of a loved one, or the presence of the divine, just to name a few. In recent years, a variety of apps have become available to help people engage in these kinds of activities 2.

2. Awe: Awe is the feeling we get when we're in the presence of a vast mystery that transcends our understanding of the world. For instance, we might feel awe in the presence of something huge, powerful, timeless, or intricate. Other people can leave us awestruck as well because of their astounding virtue, knowledge, or skill. Taking an intentional awe walk is one way we can seek awe. This might involve taking at least 15 minutes to stroll through a natural area, maybe

one that brings us through a wooded area, a field of flowers, or near a lake or river. Alternatively, we can walk under the night sky, at dawn or dusk, or while a thunderstorm takes shape in the distance. As we walk, part of the practice entails taking our time to really try to take in what we notice as vast, for example, by allowing ourselves to be swept away by a view or amazed by the detail of a flower 2.

3. Forgiveness: Forgiveness is the act of letting go of resentment or anger towards someone who has wronged us. It is a powerful tool for spiritual wellness as it helps us to move on from negative emotions and focus on positive ones 2.

4. Compassion: Compassion is the ability to feel empathy for others and to act on that empathy. It is a key component of spiritual wellness as it helps us to connect with others and to feel a sense of purpose in our lives 2.

5. Gratitude: Gratitude is the practice of being thankful for what we have in our lives. It is a powerful tool for spiritual wellness as it helps us to focus on the positive aspects of our lives and to appreciate the good things that we have 2.

These practices can be conducted individually, but they may have more impact when practiced in a community 2. I hope this helps!

Table of Contents

Chapter 1

Introduction

Welcome to this book on spiritual wellness! In this book, we'll explore how to develop a sense of purpose and meaning in life, connect with something greater than oneself, and find inner peace and fulfillment. Whether you're seeking to deepen your existing spiritual practice or embark on a new journey of self-discovery, this book offers practical tools and guidance to help you on your path.

Setting the stage for the journey

Before we dive into the details, let's take a moment to set the stage for our journey together. I invite you to find a quiet and comfortable space where you can focus your attention on this book and your own inner experiences. Take a deep breath and allow yourself to be fully present in this moment, with an open and curious mind.

Understanding the basics of spiritual wellness

Before we dive into the details, let's take a moment to set the stage for our journey together. I invite you to find a quiet and comfortable space where you can focus your attention on this book and your own inner experiences. Take a deep breath and allow yourself to be fully present in this moment, with an open and curious mind.

The purpose and goals of the book

The purpose of this book is to provide you with practical tools and guidance to develop your spiritual wellness. By the end of this book, you'll have a deeper understanding of yourself and the world around you, and a set of skills and practices to help you live a more fulfilling and meaningful life.

Some specific goals in this book you may aim to achieve include:

Increased self-awareness: To help you pay attention to your thoughts, feelings, and behaviors and how they impact your overall well-being.

Greater inner peace: Through the practice of mindfulness and meditation, to help you quiet your mind and find inner peace.

Improved relationships: By understanding yourself better, you may be able to communicate more effectively and connect more deeply with others.

A deeper sense of purpose: By exploring your beliefs and values, you may be able to gain a clearer sense of what is truly important to yourself and what you want to accomplish in life.

Increased resilience: Through learning how to overcome negative thoughts and emotions, you may be better equipped to handle life's challenges and bounce back from setbacks.

Greater appreciation for life: By practicing gratitude and mindfulness, you may learn to appreciate the present moment and find joy in everyday experiences.

A deeper understanding of spirituality: Many spiritual wellness books explore different spiritual practices and beliefs, helping you to gain a deeper understanding of their own spirituality and how to connect with something greater than themselves.

These are some possible goals that this spiritual wellness book is aimed to achieve, but ultimately the purpose and goals will depend on your perspective, and your approach to the topic.

Overview of the book's structure

This book is organized into eight chapters, each covering an important aspect of spiritual wellness. In Chapter 2, we'll explore the concept of mindfulness and its benefits, and learn specific exercises and techniques to incorporate mindfulness into our daily lives. In Chapter 3, we'll delve into the topic of self-awareness, and how to use mindfulness and other practices to cultivate a deeper understanding of ourselves. Chapter 4, will focus on the role of gratitude and compassion in spiritual wellness, and provide exercises to cultivate these qualities in our daily lives.

In Chapter 5, we'll turn our attention to the importance of nature in spiritual wellness. We'll explore different ways to connect with nature, and how to use nature as a source of inspiration and guidance. In Chapter 6, we'll explore the topic of spiritual beliefs and values, and how to cultivate a deeper understanding of our own spirituality. Chapter 7 will focus on the topic of self-care and how to prioritize our own well-being, and in Chapter 8, we'll conclude our journey with reflections on how to integrate these practices and insights into our daily lives.

I hope this overview has given you a sense of what to expect from this book. Let's continue our journey together!

Spiritual Wellness

Spiritual wellness is the process of developing a sense of purpose and meaning in one's life and connecting with something greater than oneself. It can involve exploring one's beliefs, values, and spirituality through practices such as meditation, prayer, journaling, and connecting with nature. It also encompasses understanding and connecting with the spiritual aspect of oneself, developing a sense of connection and compassion with others, and expanding one's understanding of the world and one's place in it.

It is often seen as a holistic approach to well-being, encompassing not just physical and mental health, but also emotional and spiritual well-being. It is a personal and subjective experience and can be different for everyone. Some people may find spiritual fulfillment through religious or spiritual practices, while others may find it through nature, art, or community service.

Spiritual wellness can bring a sense of peace, fulfillment, and inner strength, which can help individuals cope with life's challenges and find a deeper sense of meaning and purpose. It is an ongoing process, and individuals can work on it throughout their lifetime.

Additionally, spiritual wellness can also be cultivated through various practices such as yoga, tai chi, or qigong, which can help to align the body, mind, and spirit. Reading spiritual texts and attending workshops or retreats can also be useful in developing spiritual wellness.

It is also important to note that spiritual wellness is not limited to any specific religion or belief system, it can be practiced and cultivated by individuals from all backgrounds and walks of life.

Practicing spiritual wellness can have many benefits for one's overall well-being. It can promote feelings of inner peace, joy, and contentment, as well as reducing stress and anxiety. It can also bring a sense of meaning and purpose to one's life and help individuals to feel more connected to themselves, others, and the world around them.

Overall, spiritual wellness is a process of self-discovery and growth, and it is something that can be practiced and nurtured throughout one's lifetime. It is a journey that can help individuals to find a deeper sense of meaning and purpose in their lives, and lead to a more fulfilling and satisfying existence.

Another aspect of spiritual wellness is the sense of connection with something greater than oneself, it can be a feeling of oneness with the universe, a higher power or the divine, or a connection with the natural world. This connection can bring a sense of transcendence and a feeling of being a part of something bigger, which can be very empowering.

Practicing spiritual wellness can also promote a sense of compassion and empathy towards others and the world around us, which can lead to positive actions and contribute to the greater good.

It is also important to note that spiritual wellness is not just about feeling good, it is also about growth and self-improvement. It is not a destination, but a journey and a process of self-discovery. It requires an openness to new ideas, a willingness to question and explore one's beliefs and values, and a commitment to personal growth.

In summary, spiritual wellness encompasses a wide range of practices and ideas, and it is unique to each individual. It is the process of developing a sense of purpose and meaning in life, connecting with something greater than oneself, and promoting a sense of peace, fulfillment and inner strength. It is an ongoing journey that requires commitment, openness and a willingness to explore and grow.

CHAPTER 2

Mindfulness And Meditation

Mindfulness and meditation are two powerful tools for enhancing spiritual wellness. By practicing these techniques, individuals can cultivate a deeper sense of self-awareness, calmness, and inner peace. In this chapter, we will explore the basics of mindfulness and meditation, including their benefits, various techniques, and tips for incorporating them into daily life.

Understanding mindfulness and its benefits:

To begin, let's define mindfulness. Mindfulness is the practice of being fully present and engaged in the current moment, without judgment. It involves paying attention to our thoughts, feelings, and physical sensations, as well as the world around us. Research has shown that mindfulness has numerous benefits, including reducing stress and anxiety and depression, improving sleep quality, and enhancing cognitive function. It has also been shown to lower blood pressure and improve immune function. Also increasing focus and concentration, improving emotional regulation, and promoting a greater sense of overall well-being.

The benefits of mindfulness can be wide-ranging and include:

Reduced stress and anxiety: Mindfulness can help individuals to manage their stress and anxiety by teaching them to focus on the present moment and to let go of worries about the future or regrets about the past.

Improved Emotional Well-Being: Mindfulness can help individuals to become more aware of their emotions, which can lead to greater emotional intelligence and better emotional regulation.

Increased Focus and Concentration: Mindfulness can help individuals to improve their focus and concentration by training them to pay attention to the present moment and to stay focused on a specific task.

Better Physical Health: Mindfulness can help to reduce chronic pain, improve immune function, and lower blood pressure.

Improved Relationships: Mindfulness can help individuals to communicate more effectively, to connect more deeply with others, and to develop greater empathy.

Greater Self-Awareness: Mindfulness can help individuals to become more aware of their thoughts, feelings, and behaviors, which can lead to greater self-awareness and personal growth.

Mindfulness Exercises

These are just a few examples of mindfulness exercises and techniques that can be used to develop mindfulness skills and incorporate mindfulness into daily life. It is important to keep in mind that mindfulness is a skill that takes practice and patience, and it is important to be kind and compassionate with oneself while learning these techniques.

Mindful Breathing

Mindful breathing is a type of mindfulness meditation that involves focusing on the breath as a way to bring attention to the present moment. It is a simple and effective technique that can be practiced anywhere at any time.

To begin, find a comfortable seated position with your back straight and your feet flat on the floor. Place your hands on your lap or on your knees with your palms facing upward. Close your eyes or keep them open with a soft gaze.

Take a few deep breaths, inhaling through your nose and exhaling through your mouth. Then, allow your breath to flow naturally and begin to focus your attention on the sensation of your breath as it moves in and out of your body. Notice the rise and fall of your chest and abdomen with each inhale and exhale.

As you focus on your breath, you may notice that your mind begins to wander. This is normal and expected. When you become aware that your mind has wandered, gently bring your attention back to your breath without judgment.

Continue to focus on your breath for several minutes, or for as long as you feel comfortable. You may choose to count your breaths or silently repeat a word or phrase to help anchor your attention.

Practicing breathing mindfulness regularly can help to reduce stress, increase relaxation, and improve overall well-being.

Mindful Walking

Mindful walking is a form of meditation that involves walking slowly and intentionally while bringing awareness to the physical sensations of the body and the environment around you. It is a practice that can help to calm the mind, reduce stress and anxiety, and cultivate a sense of presence and gratitude.

To begin, find a quiet and peaceful place to walk, such as a park or a trail. Stand still and take a few deep breaths, centering yourself and bringing your attention to the present moment. Begin to walk slowly, focusing on the sensations of your feet touching the ground, the movement of your legs, and the flow of your breath.

As you walk, try to stay fully present in the experience. Notice the sights, sounds, and smells around you, and try to let go of any thoughts or distractions. If your mind starts to wander, simply bring your attention back to the physical sensations of walking and breathing.

You can also practice mindful walking with a specific intention or focus, such as cultivating gratitude or compassion. For example, you can take each step with the intention of expressing gratitude for the world around you, or of sending positive energy to those in need.

Mindful walking can be practiced for any length of time, from a few minutes to an hour or more. It is a simple and accessible way to incorporate mindfulness into your daily life, and to cultivate a deeper connection with yourself and the world around you.

J. M. Thorne

Mindful Eating

Mindful eating is a practice of paying attention to the present moment and fully experiencing the sensations, thoughts, and emotions that arise while eating. It involves bringing awareness to the food, the environment, and the experience of eating.

To practice mindful eating, begin by selecting a food item and examining it closely. Take note of its color, texture, and shape. Observe any sensations that arise in your body, such as hunger or anticipation.

Before eating, take a few deep breaths and bring your attention to the present moment. As you begin to eat, take small bites and chew slowly. Pay attention to the flavors, textures, and sensations of the food in your mouth.

If your mind begins to wander, gently bring your attention back to the present moment and the experience of eating. Avoid distractions such as watching TV or reading while eating. Instead, focus solely on the act of eating and the experience of nourishing your body.

By practicing mindful eating, you can develop a deeper appreciation for food and the act of eating. This can lead to a greater sense of satisfaction and fulfillment in your meals, as well as a healthier relationship with food.

Mindful Listening

Mindful listening is a practice that involves fully focusing on the act of listening, without any distractions or judgments. It is a powerful tool that can improve communication and relationships, as well as deepen one's understanding and appreciation of others.

To practice mindful listening, it is important to first find a quiet and comfortable space where you can focus your attention. Next, choose a person or recording to listen to, such as a friend, family member, or a podcast episode.

As you listen, make a conscious effort to pay attention to the words being spoken, the tone of voice, and the emotions behind the words. Avoid interrupting or planning your response, and instead simply listen with an open mind and heart.

You may also notice any physical sensations or emotions that arise as you listen, such as tension or empathy. Acknowledge these feelings without judgment, and continue to focus on the act of listening.

By practicing mindful listening regularly, you can improve your communication skills, deepen your relationships, and cultivate greater empathy and understanding towards others.

3 Minutes

Another mindfulness practice that can be helpful for developing mindfulness skills is the "3-minute breathing space" which can be used as a quick and easy way to bring mindfulness into your day. It involves taking 3 minutes to pause and focus on your breath and bodily sensations. You can do this by finding a comfortable seated position, closing your eyes, and bringing your attention to your breath. You can use the following steps:

Begin by noticing the sensations of your breath as it enters and leaves your body.

 Expand your awareness to include your body as a whole, noticing any sensations or areas of tension.

Allow any thoughts or emotions that arise to pass by without getting caught up in them.

After 3 minutes, take a deep breath in and out, and open your eyes.

 This practice can be done anytime during the day, and it's a great way to bring mindfulness into your daily routine and to reduce stress and anxiety.

Different Meditation Techniques and How to Practice Them

There are several different types of meditation, each with its own unique benefits and techniques. And it's important to find the one that works best for you. Some common meditation techniques include:

Mindfulness Meditation

Mindfulness meditation is a form of meditation that involves intentionally focusing your attention on the present moment without judgment. This practice is often used to reduce stress, improve mental health, and increase overall well-being. Here's how to practice mindfulness meditation:

Find a quiet and comfortable place to sit or lie down where you won't be disturbed.

Close your eyes and take a few deep breaths to relax your body and mind.

Begin by bringing your attention to your breath. Notice the sensation of air moving in and out of your nose or mouth. You can also focus on the rise and fall of your chest or belly.

When your mind starts to wander, gently bring it back to your breath without judgment or criticism.

As you continue to focus on your breath, you may notice thoughts, emotions, or physical sensations arising. Acknowledge them without judgment or attachment, and then return your attention to your breath.

Practice for a set amount of time, such as 5-10 minutes to start, and gradually increase the time as you become more comfortable with the practice.

It's important to remember that mindfulness meditation is a practice, and it takes time and patience to develop. Don't be discouraged if your mind wanders frequently or you find it difficult to stay focused at first. With consistent practice, you can train your mind to stay present and improve your overall well-being.

Body Scan Meditation

Body scan meditation is a mindfulness practice that involves systematically scanning the body from head to toe, paying attention to physical sensations and observing any tension, discomfort or sensations without judgment.

To begin a body scan meditation, find a comfortable and quiet place where you can lie down or sit comfortably. Close your eyes and take a few deep breaths, focusing your attention on the present moment.

Start at the top of your head, and slowly move your attention down your body, paying attention to any sensations you feel. You can start by focusing on your scalp, then your forehead, and then move to your face and neck.

As you continue to move down your body, observe any physical sensations without judgment or reaction. Take note of any areas of tension, discomfort or pain.

You can also practice deep breathing as you scan your body, inhaling slowly and deeply, and exhaling fully. As you exhale, imagine releasing any tension or stress from that area of your body.

Continue the body scan meditation until you reach your toes, taking your time to observe each area of your body. Once you reach your toes, take a few deep breaths and slowly open your eyes.

Body scan meditation is a great way to develop mindfulness and awareness of your body, and can help to reduce stress and tension. It can be practiced regularly as part of a mindfulness routine or as a way to relax and unwind after a long day.

The Loving-Kindness Meditation

Another mindfulness technique that can be useful is "The Loving-Kindness Meditation" also known as "Metta" which is a practice that involves cultivating feelings of love and compassion towards oneself and others. This practice can help to increase feelings of connection and compassion, and can be done by:

Sitting or standing comfortably, and closing your eyes.

Bringing to mind someone you love and silently repeating phrases of well-wishes, such as "May you be happy, may you be healthy, may you be safe, may you be at ease."

Expanding the well-wishes to include yourself, friends,

acquaintances, and all living beings.

As you repeat the phrases, try to focus on the feeling of love and compassion in your heart.

Continue the practice for a few minutes, and when you are ready, take a deep breath in and out, and open your eyes.

Transcendental Meditation

Transcendental Meditation (TM) is a specific type of meditation that involves using a mantra or sound as a focus for the mind. Here's a step-by-step guide on how to practice TM:

Choose a quiet and comfortable place to sit down where you won't be disturbed for at least 20 minutes.

Sit with your back straight and your hands in your lap, with your palms facing up.

Close your eyes and take a few deep breaths to relax your body and clear your mind.

Begin silently repeating a mantra to yourself. A mantra is a word or sound that is repeated over and over again. The mantra used in TM is given to you by a certified TM teacher and is kept private.

As you repeat the mantra, focus on the sound and let go of any thoughts or distractions that may arise. If your mind starts to wander, gently bring your attention back to the mantra.

Continue to repeat the mantra for about 20 minutes.

After 20 minutes, gradually become aware of your surroundings and your body. Take a few deep breaths before opening your eyes.

It's important to note that TM is usually learned through a certified TM teacher, who provides personalized guidance and support. They will also give you your personal mantra and teach you how to use it properly. With regular practice, TM can help reduce stress and anxiety, improve focus and concentration, and promote a sense of inner calm and well-being.

Breathing Meditation

Breathing meditation, also known as breath awareness meditation, is a type of mindfulness meditation that involves paying attention to the breath. The practice involves finding a comfortable seated position and focusing on the sensations of the breath as it moves in and out of the body.

Find a quiet place where you won't be disturbed.

Sit in a comfortable position with your back straight and your feet flat on the ground.

Close your eyes and bring your attention to your breath. Notice the sensation of the breath moving in and out of your body.

Focus on your breath. You can choose to focus on the sensation of the breath at your nostrils, the rise and fall of your chest, or the expansion and contraction of your belly.

If your mind begins to wander, gently bring your attention back to your breath. Don't judge yourself for getting distracted; it's natural for the mind to wander.

Continue to focus on your breath for a set period of time, such as 5-10 minutes.

Breathing meditation can be practiced on its own or as part of a longer meditation practice. Regular practice of breathing meditation has been shown to reduce stress and anxiety, improve sleep, and enhance overall well-being.

Yoga Meditation

Yoga meditation is a practice that combines physical postures, breath control, and meditation to cultivate inner peace, mindfulness, and a deeper connection with the self. Yoga has been used for centuries as a tool for spiritual and physical wellness, and its benefits have been well-documented.

In yoga meditation, the practitioner moves through a series of postures, or asanas, while focusing on their breath and body sensations. The movements are slow and deliberate, allowing the practitioner to connect with their body and breath in a mindful way.

As the practice progresses, the practitioner may move into seated meditation, where they focus their attention on their breath, body sensations, or a specific mantra or visualization. The goal is to quiet the mind and cultivate a sense of inner peace and awareness.

Yoga meditation has been shown to have numerous benefits for both physical and mental health, including reducing stress and anxiety, improving sleep, increasing flexibility and strength, and improving overall wellbeing. It is a powerful tool for those seeking to deepen their spiritual practice and improve their overall health and wellness.

5 Minutes

Another practice that can be helpful is the "5 senses meditation" which involves paying attention to each of the five senses in turn: sight, sound, touch, taste, and smell. This practice can help to increase awareness and focus, and can be done by:

Sitting or standing comfortably, and closing your eyes.

Bringing your attention to each of your five senses in turn.

Noticing any sensations or feelings that arise, and trying to observe them without judgment.

These are just a few examples of mindfulness exercises and techniques that can be used to develop mindfulness skills and incorporate mindfulness into daily life. It is important to keep in mind that mindfulness is a skill that takes practice and patience, and it is important to be kind and compassionate with oneself while learning these techniques.

Incorporating Mindfulness and Meditation into Daily Life

The key to incorporating mindfulness and meditation into daily life is to make it a regular habit. This can involve setting aside a specific time each day to practice, or integrating mindfulness into everyday activities such as walking, eating, or even washing the dishes.

It's also important to be patient and gentle with yourself when starting a mindfulness or meditation practice. It's natural for the mind to wander, and it can take time to develop the habit of being present in the moment. With regular practice, however, individuals can cultivate a greater sense of inner peace and clarity, and experience the numerous benefits of mindfulness and meditation.

CHAPTER 3

Connecting With Nature

The Importance Of Nature in Spiritual Wellness

Nature plays an essential role in spiritual wellness. Connecting with nature can bring us a sense of peace, awe, and wonder that can help us feel grounded, centered, and connected with the world around us. In today's fast-paced and technology-driven world, many of us spend most of our time indoors and disconnected from the natural world. This disconnection can leave us feeling stressed, anxious, and spiritually disconnected.

Nature has the power to heal and restore our spiritual wellness. Spending time in nature can help us slow down, relax, and let go of our worries and distractions. It can provide us with a sense of perspective, reminding us that we are just a small part of a vast and interconnected universe. When we immerse ourselves in nature, we can tap into a deep sense of gratitude and appreciation for the beauty and diversity of life.

In addition to providing us with a sense of peace and wonder, nature can also serve as a source of inspiration and guidance. Many spiritual traditions view nature as a sacred and divine creation, filled with lessons and teachings for those who seek them. By observing the natural world, we can learn valuable lessons about impermanence, balance, and interconnectedness. We can also find guidance and insight by tuning into the rhythms and cycles of nature, which reflect the cycles of our own lives.

Nature can help us cultivate a deeper sense of spiritual wellness by providing us with a sense of peace, wonder, and connection. It can also serve as a source of inspiration and guidance, helping us to learn important lessons about ourselves and the world around us.

Connecting with nature can be a powerful tool in promoting spiritual wellness. The natural world has been proven to have a calming effect on the mind and body, and can help to reduce stress, anxiety, and depression. It can also help to provide a sense of perspective and remind us of our place in the world.

Spending time in nature can be as simple as taking a walk in a park or a hike in the woods. Engaging in activities such as gardening, bird watching, or stargazing can also help to foster a deeper connection with the natural world. Additionally, practicing mindfulness while in nature can help to increase our awareness and appreciation of our surroundings.

Incorporating nature into our spiritual practice can also help to provide a sense of connection with something greater than ourselves. Many spiritual traditions view nature as a manifestation of the divine, and spending time in nature can help to connect us with this spiritual energy.

Furthermore, nature can serve as a source of inspiration and guidance. The natural world is filled with examples of resilience, adaptability, and growth, and can provide valuable lessons for our own spiritual journeys. Whether we are learning to let go of the past, to embrace change, or to find beauty in unexpected places, nature can offer us the guidance and wisdom we need to move forward.

In summary, connecting with nature is an important aspect of spiritual wellness. It can help to promote feelings of calm and relaxation, foster a sense of connection with something greater than ourselves, and provide valuable lessons and guidance for our spiritual journeys.

Different Ways To Connect With Nature

Connecting with nature can take many different forms, and the best approach will depend on your personal preferences and interests. Here are some different ways you can connect with nature:

Spend Time In Natural Environments

One of the simplest and most effective ways to connect with nature is simply to spend time in natural environments. This could involve going for a walk in the woods, hiking in the mountains, or swimming in a lake. By immersing yourself in the natural world, you can experience the sights, sounds, and sensations of the environment, and develop a deeper appreciation for the natural world.

Gardening

Gardening is a great way to connect with nature on a more intimate level. Whether you have a small garden or a large plot of land, gardening can provide an opportunity to cultivate a deeper understanding of the natural world. Through the process of planting, nurturing, and harvesting, you can develop a sense of connection to the cycles of growth and change that occur in the natural world.

Wildlife Observation

Another way to connect with nature is through wildlife observation. This could involve watching birds at a bird feeder, observing animals in the wild, or simply paying attention to the insects and other small creatures that you encounter in your daily life. By observing the behavior and habits of animals, you can gain a deeper understanding of the interconnectedness of all living things.

Outdoor Recreation

Outdoor recreation: Outdoor recreation activities such as camping, fishing, and kayaking can also provide opportunities to connect with nature. By engaging in these activities, you can experience the natural world in a more active and immersive way, and develop a deeper appreciation for the beauty and power of nature.

Creative Expression

Finally, creative expression can be a powerful way to connect with nature. Whether through painting, writing, or other forms of artistic expression, engaging with nature in a creative way can help to deepen your connection to the natural world and provide a sense of peace and fulfillment.

Nature has been a source of inspiration and guidance for people throughout history. From poets and artists to scientists and spiritual leaders, many have found inspiration and guidance in the natural world. There is something about being in nature that can help us connect with our deeper selves, our purpose, and our spirituality.

For some, nature can be a source of awe and wonder. The beauty and majesty of mountains, oceans, and forests can inspire feelings of humility, gratitude, and reverence. For others, nature can be a place of peace and tranquility. The quiet, stillness, and simplicity of nature can help us to slow down, breathe deeply, and find inner calm.

In addition to providing inspiration and peace, nature can also be a source of guidance. Nature has a way of showing us the interconnectedness of all things, and can teach us valuable lessons about life and spirituality. For example, observing the cycles of the seasons or the ebb and flow of the tides can remind us of the impermanence of life and the importance of embracing change.

J. M. Thorne

Moreover, many spiritual traditions have incorporated nature into their practices and beliefs. For example, in indigenous cultures, nature is often viewed as a living entity, with which we can communicate and build relationships. In many Eastern religions, such as Buddhism and Taoism, nature is seen as a manifestation of the divine and a teacher of spiritual truths.

Overall, the importance of nature in spiritual wellness cannot be overstated. Whether it is through hiking in the mountains, walking along the beach, or simply sitting in a park, spending time in nature can help us to connect with our inner selves, find inspiration and guidance, and deepen our spiritual practices.

The Nature Walk Meditation

Another mindfulness technique that can be useful is "The Nature Walk Meditation" which involves taking a walk in nature and paying attention to the sights, sounds, and sensations of the natural environment. This practice can help to increase awareness and reduce stress and anxiety. It can be done by:

Finding a nearby park or nature trail.

Taking a walk and paying attention to the sights, sounds, and sensations of the natural environment around you.

Notice the different colors, the textures, and the smells of nature.

Take note of the different animals, trees, and plants that you see and hear.

As you walk, try to focus on the present moment, and let go of any thoughts or worries about the future or past.

After your walk, take a few minutes to reflect on your experience and the feelings that came up for you.

Another practice that can be helpful is "The Yoga Practice" which combines physical postures, breathing techniques, and meditation to help bring balance to the body and mind. Practicing yoga regularly can help to increase flexibility, strength, and balance, as well as reducing stress and anxiety.

It's important to remember that these practices aren't a one-size-fits-all solution and it's always good to try different techniques and find what works best for you. As you try different practices and techniques, be sure to pay attention to how they make you feel, and continue with the ones that resonate with you the most. Remember, the key is to make mindfulness a regular part of your life, not just a one-time event.

CHAPTER 4

Self-Awareness & Self-Discovery

Self-awareness and self-discovery are essential components of spiritual wellness. Self-awareness is the ability to recognize and understand one's emotions, thoughts, and behaviors. It is the first step towards self-discovery, which is the process of gaining a deeper understanding of oneself, including one's values, beliefs, strengths, weaknesses, and purpose in life.

Through self-awareness and self-discovery, individuals can identify the areas of their lives that require attention and growth. This process can help them recognize and overcome negative patterns of thinking and behavior that may be holding them back from achieving their goals and living a fulfilling life.

Self-awareness and self-discovery can be achieved through various practices, such as meditation, journaling, self-reflection, and therapy. These practices can help individuals connect with their inner selves, explore their feelings and thoughts, and gain insight into their strengths and weaknesses.

By becoming more self-aware, individuals can also develop a greater sense of empathy and understanding towards others. They can learn to communicate more effectively and form deeper, more meaningful connections with those around them.

Self-discovery is also a key component of understanding the self. Self-discovery involves exploring our interests, passions, and strengths, and discovering new things about ourselves. This can involve trying new activities, learning new skills, or simply taking time to reflect on our experiences and what we have learned.

Overall, self-awareness and self-discovery are critical components of spiritual wellness as they help individuals to develop a deeper understanding of themselves and the world around them, leading to a more fulfilling and purposeful life.

Understanding The Self

Understanding the self is a crucial aspect of spiritual wellness. It involves developing self-awareness, which is the ability to observe and understand your thoughts, emotions, and behaviors in the present moment. Self-awareness allows you to recognize your strengths and weaknesses, your values and beliefs, and your desires and goals. It is the foundation of personal growth and self-improvement. This can be cultivated through mindfulness practices, such as meditation, journaling, or simply taking time to reflect on our experiences.

To understand the self, it is essential to practice self-reflection. Self-reflection involves taking the time to look inward and evaluate your thoughts, emotions, and behaviors. It allows you to gain a deeper

                                                        J. M. Thorne

understanding of yourself and your experiences. Self-reflection can be done through journaling, meditation, or simply taking a few moments each day to reflect on your experiences.

Another aspect of understanding the self is exploring our beliefs and values. Our beliefs and values shape the way we see the world and the decisions we make. By exploring our beliefs and values, we can gain a better understanding of our motivations and goals, and make decisions that align with our authentic selves. Your values are the things that are most important to you, such as honesty, compassion, or creativity. Your beliefs are the ideas and assumptions that shape your worldview. By identifying your values and beliefs, you can gain insight into your motivations and behaviors.

Finally, it is essential to practice self-acceptance as a part of understanding the self. Self-acceptance involves embracing all aspects of yourself, including your flaws and imperfections. It is about recognizing that you are a unique individual with your own strengths and weaknesses. By practicing self-acceptance, you can develop a positive self-image and a greater sense of self-worth.

Overall, understanding the self is a lifelong process that involves developing self-awareness, exploring your values and beliefs, and practicing self-acceptance. It is an essential aspect of spiritual wellness that can lead to personal growth and a deeper connection with yourself and the world around you.

Beliefs & Values

Exploring beliefs and values is an essential aspect of spiritual wellness. It involves examining one's personal beliefs and values and how they influence thoughts, feelings, and actions. Our beliefs and values guide our behavior and decision-making, and exploring them can lead to a better understanding of oneself and the world around us.

One way to explore beliefs and values is to reflect on personal experiences and identify the underlying beliefs and values that influenced those experiences. For example, if you recently experienced a setback, reflect on what beliefs or values may have contributed to that setback. Maybe you believed that you were not capable of achieving the task, or maybe you valued immediate results over long-term success.

Another way to explore beliefs and values is to examine how they compare with societal or cultural norms. It is important to consider whether our beliefs and values are truly our own, or if they have been influenced by outside factors such as family, friends, or media. This process of reflection can help identify any conflicting beliefs and values, leading to personal growth and a better understanding of oneself.

It is also essential to recognize that beliefs and values can change over time. As we grow and have new experiences, our perspectives and beliefs may shift. It is important to regularly assess our beliefs and values and be open to change.

By exploring beliefs and values, we can develop a deeper understanding of ourselves, our motivations, and our behaviors. This can lead to personal growth, greater self-awareness, and improved relationships with others. It can also help us align our actions with our values, leading to a more fulfilling and meaningful life.

Journaling For Self-Discovery

Journaling is a simple yet powerful technique for self-discovery that can help individuals explore their thoughts, feelings, and experiences. Through the act of writing, individuals can gain insight into their inner world and uncover patterns, beliefs, and emotions that may be influencing their behavior and decisions.

To start journaling for self-discovery, it is helpful to set aside a regular time and place for writing, where there are no distractions or interruptions. This can be a few minutes each day, or longer periods of time on a weekly basis.

Begin by writing freely and spontaneously about whatever comes to mind, without worrying about grammar, spelling, or punctuation. It can be helpful to write about a specific event or experience, or to reflect on a particular emotion or issue that is on your mind.

As you continue to journal, you may start to notice themes or patterns in your writing. You may discover underlying beliefs or values that are driving your thoughts and behaviors, or you may gain insight into patterns of behavior that are holding you back or causing you stress.

Journaling can also be a useful tool for problem-solving and decision-making. By writing down your thoughts and options, you can clarify your thinking and gain a fresh perspective on the situation.

In addition to written journaling, there are many other creative ways to explore your inner world, such as drawing, painting, or collage-making. These activities can help you tap into your intuition and express yourself in a nonverbal way.

Overall, journaling and other creative techniques for self-discovery can help individuals deepen their understanding of themselves and their inner world, and can lead to greater self-awareness and personal growth.

Here are some affirmations you can use for journaling

I am capable of achieving my goals.

I am worthy of love and respect.

I trust in the universe to guide me towards my highest good.

I release all negative energy and embrace positivity.

I am grateful for all the blessings in my life.

I forgive myself and others for any past mistakes or wrongdoings.

I am confident in my abilities and strengths.

I am open to new opportunities and experiences.

I am deserving of happiness and fulfillment.

I am at peace with myself and the world around me.

Remember to choose affirmations that resonate with you and your personal goals, and to write them in the present tense to reinforce positive thinking and beliefs.

CHAPTER 5

Overcoming Negative Thoughts & Emotions

Overcoming negative thoughts and emotions. In this chapter, we will be exploring the different ways in which we can manage and overcome negative thoughts and emotions that may hinder our spiritual wellness journey.

Negative thoughts and emotions can arise from various factors such as past experiences, current situations, and the people we surround ourselves with. These thoughts and emotions can have a significant impact on our mental and emotional well-being, making it difficult for us to feel at peace and happy.

However, it's important to remember that we have the power to control our thoughts and emotions, and we can learn to overcome them through various techniques and practices. In this chapter, we will explore some of these techniques and practices, and how you can incorporate them into your daily life to improve your spiritual wellness.

Understanding Negative Thoughts & Emotions

Negative thoughts and emotions are a natural part of human experience. They can arise due to various reasons such as stress, anxiety, fear, or past experiences. Negative thoughts and emotions can be a significant challenge for individuals, and if left unchecked, they can lead to mental and emotional distress, affecting one's overall well-being.

To understand negative thoughts and emotions, it is essential to recognize the role they play in our lives. Negative thoughts and emotions can serve as warning signals that something is wrong or needs attention. For example, feelings of anxiety and stress may indicate that one is facing a challenging situation or needs to take a break from work. Negative emotions can also help individuals develop greater empathy and understanding towards others who may be experiencing similar feelings.

However, negative thoughts and emotions can also be harmful when they become persistent and overwhelming. They can lead to a negative outlook on life, a decrease in self-esteem, and even depression. Therefore, it is important to learn how to manage negative thoughts and emotions effectively.

By understanding the underlying causes of negative thoughts and emotions, individuals can gain insight into their patterns of thinking and develop strategies to overcome them. Mindfulness practices such as meditation, breathing exercises, and journaling can help individuals become more aware of their thoughts and feelings, enabling them to respond to them more effectively.

Overall, understanding negative thoughts and emotions is the first step towards managing them effectively. By developing self-awareness and a deeper understanding of one's thoughts and feelings, individuals can take control of their emotions and lead a more fulfilling life.

Techniques For Managing Negative Thoughts & Emotions

Negative thoughts and emotions are a natural part of the human experience, but when left unchecked, they can become overwhelming and even debilitating. The good news is that there are many techniques you can use to manage negative thoughts and emotions. Here are some of the most effective ones:

Cognitive Restructuring

This technique involves identifying and challenging negative thoughts and beliefs that are not serving you well. By replacing these negative thoughts with more positive and empowering ones, you can begin to shift your perspective and feel more in control of your thoughts and emotions.

Mindfulness Meditation

Mindfulness meditation is a powerful tool for managing negative thoughts and emotions. It involves becoming aware of your thoughts and emotions without judging or reacting to them. This can help you develop a greater sense of inner peace and calm, even in the face of difficult emotions.

Gratitude Practice

Practicing gratitude involves focusing on the positive aspects of your life and cultivating a sense of appreciation for them. By regularly acknowledging the things you are grateful for, you can shift your focus away from negative thoughts and emotions and begin to cultivate a more positive mindset.

Exercise

Exercise is a great way to manage negative thoughts and emotions. Physical activity releases endorphins, which are feel-good chemicals that can help to improve your mood and reduce feelings of stress and anxiety.

Creative Expression

Engaging in creative activities like writing, drawing, or painting can be a powerful way to manage negative thoughts and emotions. By expressing yourself creatively, you can release pent-up emotions and gain new insights into your thoughts and feelings.

Social Support

Connecting with others who understand what you are going through can be a powerful way to manage negative thoughts and emotions.

Whether through therapy, support groups, or simply spending time with friends and family, social support can help you feel less alone and more resilient in the face of difficult emotions.

Self-Compassion

Finally, practicing self-compassion is key to managing negative thoughts and emotions. This involves treating yourself with the same kindness and understanding that you would offer to a close friend. By practicing self-compassion, you can begin to let go of self-criticism and cultivate a more positive and nurturing relationship with yourself.

Cultivating Positive Thoughts & Emotions

Cultivating positive thoughts and emotions involves intentionally shifting our mindset towards more positive and optimistic thinking. This can have a profound impact on our overall well-being and quality of life. Here are some techniques to help cultivate positive thoughts and emotions.

Gratitude

Practicing gratitude involves intentionally focusing on the things in our lives that we are thankful for. This can be done through journaling, making mental notes of things we appreciate throughout the day, or expressing gratitude to others.

Positive Self-Talk

Our inner dialogue can have a powerful impact on our mood and outlook on life. Practice replacing negative self-talk with positive affirmations and self-talk. For example, instead of thinking "I can't do this", try thinking "I am capable and strong".

Mindfulness

Mindfulness practices can help us become more aware of our thoughts and emotions, and can also help us develop a more accepting and non-judgmental attitude towards ourselves and others. This can involve practices like meditation, breathing exercises, and mindful movement.

Acts of kindness

Doing something kind for others can give us a sense of purpose and fulfillment, as well as boost our mood and sense of connection with others.

Positive visualization

Visualizing positive outcomes and experiences can help us cultivate a more optimistic mindset. This can involve visualizing ourselves achieving our goals, imagining ourselves in happy and fulfilling situations, and focusing on positive emotions like joy and contentment.

It's important to remember that cultivating positive thoughts and emotions is a practice, and it may take time and effort to develop these habits. However, with consistent effort, these techniques can have a powerful impact on our overall well-being and sense of happiness.

CHAPTER 6

Finding Purpose & Meaning In Life

In this chapter, we will explore the importance of finding purpose and meaning in life for spiritual wellness. Many of us may feel lost or unsure about our purpose in life, which can lead to feelings of dissatisfaction and a lack of fulfillment. By discovering our purpose and meaning, we can tap into our innermost desires and create a more meaningful and fulfilling life.

This chapter will provide guidance on how to identify your purpose and meaning in life, as well as techniques for incorporating them into your daily routine. We will also explore the benefits of living a purposeful life and how it can positively impact your spiritual wellness.

The Importance Of Having A Sense Of Purpose

Having a sense of purpose is important because it provides direction and meaning in life. When we have a clear sense of what we want to achieve and what we value, we are better able to make decisions and prioritize our time and energy. Without a sense of purpose, we may feel aimless, unfulfilled, and unsure about what we want from life. This can lead to feelings of boredom, frustration, and even depression.

 Having a sense of purpose can also help us to stay motivated, even in difficult times. When we encounter obstacles or setbacks, knowing that we are working towards a meaningful goal can give us the strength and determination to keep going. Additionally, having a sense of purpose can help us to connect with others who share our values and goals, leading to a greater sense of community and belonging.

Exploring Different Paths To Finding Purpose & Meaning

 Exploring different paths to finding purpose and meaning can be a meaningful and fulfilling experience. It involves taking the time to reflect on your passions, values, and interests in order to find a sense of direction and purpose in life. Here are some ways to explore different paths to finding purpose and meaning:

Self-Reflection

Take some time to reflect on what brings you joy, what you are passionate about, and what values you hold most dear. These are often good starting points in exploring your purpose and meaning.

Seeking Inspiration from Others

Look for role models and people you admire who are living purposeful and meaningful lives. Take inspiration from their journeys and use their stories as a guide to help you find your own path.

Exploring New Opportunities

Don't be afraid to try new things and explore new opportunities. Take a class, join a group, or take on a new project that aligns with your interests and passions.

Volunteering

Volunteering can be a great way to find purpose and meaning in life. It can help you feel a sense of connection to your community and make a positive impact on the lives of others.

Spiritual Practices

Engage in spiritual practices that help you connect with something greater than yourself. This could include meditation, prayer, or other rituals that help you feel more connected and grounded.

By exploring these different paths, you may be able to find a greater sense of purpose and meaning in life. It's important to remember that the journey

Setting & Achieving Personal Goals

Take Action

Taking action is the most crucial step in achieving your goals. Make a habit of working towards your goals every day, even if it's just a small step forward.

Setting and achieving personal goals is an essential aspect of finding purpose and meaning in life. It involves identifying what you want to achieve and taking concrete steps to make those aspirations a reality. Here's how to set and achieve personal goals:

Define your Goals

The first step in setting personal goals is to determine what you want to achieve. Be specific about your goals and ensure that they are realistic and achievable.

Write them Down

Writing your goals down makes them more tangible and gives you a sense of accountability. Keep your goals in a visible place where you can see them daily, such as on your phone, computer, or a piece of paper on your desk.

Break them Down

Break your larger goals into smaller, more manageable steps. This will help you stay motivated and focused on making progress. It also makes it easier to track your progress and celebrate your achievements.

Develop a Plan

Once you've broken your goals down into smaller steps, create a plan for how you'll achieve each one. This might include deadlines, milestones, or specific actions you'll take to get there.

Stay Accountable

Hold yourself accountable for your progress by tracking your achievements and setbacks. This will help you stay motivated and on track towards your goals.

Celebrate your Successes

Celebrate each success, no matter how small. This will help you stay motivated and build momentum towards achieving your larger goals.

By following these steps, you can set and achieve personal goals that help you find purpose and meaning in your life. Remember, the journey towards achieving your goals may not always be easy, but the sense of accomplishment and fulfillment you'll gain from reaching them will make it all worth it.

J. M. Thorne

CHAPTER 7

Gratitude & Appreciation

Gratitude and appreciation are two important elements that contribute significantly to our well-being and happiness. Practicing gratitude can bring about positive changes in our lives, such as reducing stress, increasing resilience, improving relationships, and promoting a positive outlook on life. By focusing on the good things in our lives and being grateful for them, we can learn to appreciate what we have and find happiness in the present moment.

This chapter will explore the concept of gratitude and appreciation, and provide practical tips and techniques for cultivating a sense of gratitude in our daily lives. We will discuss the benefits of gratitude, the science behind it, and how to practice gratitude and appreciation to live a more fulfilling and meaningful life.

Understanding The Power Of Gratitude

Gratitude is the act of acknowledging and appreciating the good things in our lives. It is the recognition of the positive aspects of life and being thankful for them. Practicing gratitude has been shown to have many benefits, including reducing stress, improving relationships, and enhancing overall well-being.

One reason gratitude is so powerful is because it helps shift our focus from what is lacking in our lives to what we do have. When we focus on the good things, we naturally feel more positive and content. This positive mindset can also help us cope with difficult situations and challenges.

In addition to improving our mental and emotional well-being, gratitude can also have physical benefits. Studies have shown that practicing gratitude can improve sleep, lower blood pressure, and boost the immune system.

Overall, gratitude is a simple but powerful practice that can have a significant impact on our lives. By taking the time to appreciate the good things, we can cultivate a sense of abundance and contentment, and improve our overall health and well-being.

Incorporating Gratitude Into Daily Life

Incorporating gratitude into our daily lives can be a powerful tool for increasing our overall sense of well-being and happiness. Here are some ways to practice gratitude:

Keep a gratitude journal

Each day, take a few minutes to write down three to five things that you are grateful for. These can be big or small things, like a warm cup of coffee or a good conversation with a friend.

Express gratitude to others

Take the time to thank someone who has done something kind for you, whether it's a friend who has listened to you vent or a coworker who has helped you with a project.

Practice mindfulness

Pay attention to the present moment and focus on what you are grateful for in that moment. This could be as simple as noticing the beauty of a flower or the feeling of sunshine on your skin.

Use visual reminders

Place visual reminders of gratitude around your home or workspace, such as a gratitude jar where you can add notes about things you are grateful for, or a gratitude board where you can post pictures or quotes that inspire gratitude.

Reframe negative situations

When faced with a negative situation, try to find the silver lining and focus on what you can learn or gain from the experience.

Practice gratitude during meals

Take a moment before eating to express gratitude for the food and those who prepared it. This can help cultivate a sense of mindfulness and appreciation for the simple things in life.

Incorporating these practices into your daily routine can help shift your focus toward the positive aspects of your life and increase your overall sense of happiness and well-being.

Finding Joy In Everyday Experiences

Finding joy in everyday experiences is an essential aspect of cultivating a more positive and fulfilling life. It is a mindset that involves focusing on the present moment, being mindful of your surroundings, and finding the beauty and joy in small moments.

Here are some ways to find joy in everyday experiences:

Be Present

Practice mindfulness and focus on the present moment. Let go of distractions and be fully engaged in what you are doing.

Find Beauty in Small Things

Look around you and notice the small details that you might usually overlook. It could be the color of the sky, the way the sun shines through the leaves, or the sound of birds chirping.

Engage your Senses

Pay attention to your senses and how they interact with your environment. Take in the sights, sounds, smells, and textures around you.

Practice Gratitude

Make a habit of acknowledging and appreciating the good things in your life. Take time each day to reflect on what you are grateful for.

Try Something New

Step out of your comfort zone and try something new, whether it's a new hobby, food, or activity. This can help you see the world in a new way and find joy in unexpected places.

Connect with Others

Spend time with people you care about, or make an effort to connect with new people. Engaging in meaningful conversations and sharing experiences with others can bring a sense of joy and fulfillment to your life.

By cultivating a mindset of joy and appreciation, you can learn to find happiness in even the most mundane moments of your day. Remember that joy is not something that is out of reach – it is a state of mind that can be cultivated with practice and intention.

The Gratitude Practice

Another practice that can be helpful is "The Gratitude Practice" which involves taking time to reflect on the things you are grateful for in your life. This practice can help to increase positive emotions and reduce stress and anxiety. It can be done by:

Setting aside a few minutes each day to reflect on the things you are grateful for.

Writing them down in a journal or sharing them with someone else.

Reflect on how these things have positively impacted your life.

As you reflect, try to focus on the feelings of gratitude and appreciation in your heart.

These are just a few examples of mindfulness exercises and techniques that can be used to develop mindfulness skills and incorporate mindfulness into daily life. The key is to find the practices that resonate with you and to make them a part of your daily routine. Remember to be patient and kind with yourself as you learn and practice these techniques, and most importantly, enjoy the journey.

CHAPTER 8

Conclusion

Congratulations! You have now reached the end of this book on spiritual wellness. Over the course of this book, we have explored various topics related to spiritual wellness, including mindfulness, self-awareness, overcoming negative thoughts and emotions, finding purpose and meaning in life, and the power of gratitude.

Throughout the book, we have discussed the importance of taking care of our spiritual well-being, and how it is an integral part of our overall health and happiness. By cultivating a greater sense of mindfulness, self-awareness, and gratitude, we can learn to live more fulfilling and purposeful lives.

As we conclude this book, I want to emphasize that the journey towards spiritual wellness is a lifelong one. It requires commitment, patience, and practice. It is not something that can be achieved overnight, but rather a gradual process of self-discovery and growth.

I hope that the information and techniques presented in this book have been helpful in your own journey towards spiritual wellness. Remember, this is your journey, and you have the power to shape it in any way that you choose. Keep an open mind, be kind to yourself, and embrace the journey ahead.

Putting It All Together

Putting it all together means incorporating all the concepts and practices discussed in the previous chapters into your daily life. Spiritual wellness is not a one-time achievement, but a lifelong journey of personal growth and development.

To put it all together, start by reflecting on your current state of spiritual wellness. Ask yourself what aspects you want to improve and where you want to focus your efforts. Consider setting specific, achievable goals to work towards.

Next, incorporate mindfulness and meditation into your daily routine. Choose techniques that resonate with you, and practice them consistently. This can include breathing exercises, body scan meditation, mindful walking, and mindful eating.

Connecting with nature is also an essential part of spiritual wellness. Spend time in nature regularly, and find ways to appreciate and connect with the natural world around you. This can include going for a hike, meditating outdoors, or simply spending time in a park or garden.

To cultivate self-awareness and self-discovery, explore your beliefs and values. Journaling is an excellent tool for this, as it allows you to explore your thoughts and feelings in a safe and private space.

Managing negative thoughts and emotions is also crucial for spiritual wellness. Techniques such as cognitive reframing, positive self-talk, and emotional regulation can help you manage negative emotions effectively.

Finding purpose and meaning is another key aspect of spiritual wellness. Consider exploring different paths to finding your purpose, including volunteering, learning new skills, or pursuing a passion.

Finally, cultivate gratitude and appreciation in your daily life. Take time to notice and appreciate the positive experiences in your life, no matter how small they may seem.

Putting it all together takes time and effort, but the rewards are worth it. By incorporating these practices into your daily life, you can experience greater peace, fulfillment, and spiritual wellness.

Maintaining Spiritual Wellness

Maintaining spiritual wellness requires continuous effort and commitment. Here are some strategies to help you stay on track:

Practice Mindfulness

Mindfulness practices such as meditation, yoga, and deep breathing help you stay in the present moment, reduce stress and anxiety, and enhance your overall well-being.

Connect with Nature

Spending time in nature helps you cultivate a sense of peace, calm, and tranquility. Whether it's a walk in the park, a hike in the mountains, or simply sitting outside in your garden, make time to connect with the natural world.

Reflect on Your Beliefs and Values

Reflecting on your beliefs and values helps you understand what's important to you and what motivates you. It also helps you stay true to yourself and your convictions.

Set Realistic Goals

Setting realistic goals that align with your values and purpose helps you stay motivated and focused. Break down your goals into smaller, more manageable steps, and celebrate your progress along the way.

Cultivate Gratitude

Cultivating gratitude helps you appreciate the good things in your life, even when things aren't going well. Take time each day to reflect on the things you're grateful for, whether it's a warm cup of coffee, a kind gesture from a friend, or the beauty of nature.

Practice Self-Care

Taking care of yourself is essential to maintaining spiritual wellness. This means getting enough sleep, eating well, staying active, and engaging in activities that bring you joy and fulfillment.

Seek Support

Finally, don't be afraid to seek support when you need it. Whether it's from a friend, family member, or mental health professional, reaching out for help is a sign of strength, not weakness.

By incorporating these practices into your daily life, you can maintain your spiritual wellness and continue to grow and thrive as a person.

Additional Resources & Support

If you're interested in exploring spiritual wellness further, there are many resources and sources of support available. Here are a few options to consider:

Spiritual or Religious Communities

Many people find that joining a spiritual or religious community provides them with a sense of belonging and support, as well as opportunities to deepen their understanding and practice of spirituality.

Self-help Books and Resources

There are many self-help books and online resources available that offer guidance on spiritual practices, mindfulness, and personal growth. Some popular titles include "The Power of Now" by Eckhart Tolle, "The Four Agreements" by Don Miguel Ruiz, and "A New Earth" by Eckhart Tolle.

Therapy and Counseling

If you're struggling with emotional or psychological issues that are interfering with your spiritual growth, therapy or counseling may be helpful. A mental health professional can help you work through negative emotions and thought patterns, and provide guidance on developing a spiritual practice that's right for you.

Meditation and Mindfulness Classes

Many yoga studios, community centers, and meditation centers offer classes and workshops on mindfulness and meditation. These can be great opportunities to learn new techniques and connect with like-minded individuals.

Nature and Outdoor Activities

Spending time in nature and engaging in outdoor activities can be a powerful way to connect with your spirituality and promote overall well-being. Consider hiking, camping, or simply taking a walk in a park or nature preserve.

Remember, there's no one "right" way to practice spirituality, and what works for one person may not work for another. It's important to explore different techniques and approaches until you find what resonates with you. And don't be afraid to ask for help and support along the way!

Note